THE PONY CLUB

The Pony Club
Stoneleigh Park
Kenilworth
Warwickshire
CV8 2RW

Website: www.pcuk.org

The Pony Club Pocket Guide to Equestrian Dress
is published by The Pony Club

© 2013 The Pony Club
Text © 2013 Judith Draper
Illustrations © 2013 Dondi

British Library Cataloguing in Publication Data.
A catalogue record for this book is available from the British Library.

ISBN 978-1-907279-16-4

Design and Production: Paul G. Harding

Printed by Halstan Printing Group in Amersham, UK
www.halstan.co.uk

Trade distribution by Kenilworth Press
An imprint of Quiller Publishing Ltd.
Wykey House, Wykey, Shrewsbury, SY4 1JA
Tel: 01939 261616 Fax: 01939 261606
E-mail: info@quillerbooks.com
Website: www.kenilworthpress.co.uk

The Pony Club Pocket Guide to
Equestrian Dress

by Judith Draper

Contents

Rules are amended more quickly than this book can be reprinted, so before setting out to compete or take part in a particular sport or discipline, *always* check the current rulebook to make sure that you comply with the rules and regulations.

Introduction

Riding clothes, like all sportswear, are based on practical design considerations combined with a certain amount of fashion. They have always been governed by the materials available, but modern technology has made possible some great steps forward—especially in the field of safety. Every form of horsemanship, from riding indoors or hacking on an overcrowded road to jumping fixed obstacles at speed, involves a certain degree of danger. Safety should therefore be a priority when considering what to wear when riding or working around horses and ponies. Everyone who rides—at whatever level—is urged to wear the best safety gear available at all times.

Safety standards are constantly being improved, so it is wise to keep in touch with all of the latest developments and to update and upgrade your equipment to ensure that you are protected as much as possible.

Part 1
Clothes for the Job

Riding is an athletic pastime. When the horse is on the move the rider's body is constantly moving, too. The faster the paces and the more jumping, the more energetic the rider's movements. Clothes must therefore be designed to 'give' with those movements if they are to be comfortable and not restrict the rider or simply come apart at the seams.

Nowadays there is a bewildering range of suitable clothing available to the rider. The range is constantly changing and growing as new materials come on the market and as people's needs alter because of developments in their sports. There are clothes to suit all pockets and although the more expensive ones will generally last longer, there are plenty of budget-priced items that will do the job perfectly well.

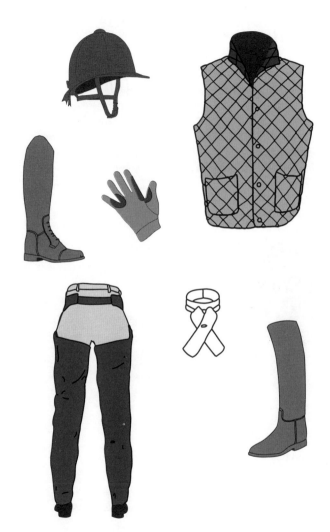

Footwear

Riding boots are designed to provide comfort, ease of movement and, most important, safety. A smooth sole and well-defined, square-cut heel minimise the risk of a rider's foot becoming trapped in the stirrup iron in the event of a fall. Thick tread and ridged soles are not allowed for riding.

Jodhpur boots, as their name implies, are ideal for wearing with jodhpurs. Unlike rubber boots (which are not suitable for younger children) they allow maximum flexibility of the ankle. They can be used for everyday riding and yard work, and are ideal for mounted games, when riders often spend some of the time dismounted and running beside their ponies.

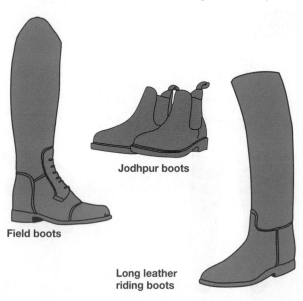

Jodhpur boots

Field boots

Long leather riding boots

Long riding boots are worn with breeches and may be made of leather or rubber. The leg should fit as closely as possible, though it is worth remembering that in cold winter weather you might want to wear thick socks or tights under your breeches or to insert an inner sole for warmth. Long boots should cover the length of the calf but must not impede the knee-joint when it is fully bent.

Alternatives to leather or rubber boots are Newmarket boots, which have canvas tops, and field boots, which have laces at the ankle. Both are suitable for riding.

If long boots are fitted with garter straps, these should be worn with the buckle positioned towards the front of the knee, against the seam of the breeches. The free end of the strap should point outwards. Over-long straps should be trimmed to about 1.5cm (½in) beyond the last keeper.

Hats

A well-fitting hat is absolutely essential and the most important item of equipment for all riders. Hats—and advice on how to choose an appropriate one—are dealt with in more detail in the chapter on **Safety** (*see* pages 24 to 29).

Legwear

Close-fitting legwear is an essential part of riding kit. It protects the skin from being chafed through constant contact with the saddle and stirrup leathers.

Jodhpurs and breeches are the traditional items of legwear, but nowadays there is also a wide range of specially designed riding trousers on the market. These are often cheaper than jodhpurs and are therefore very useful for everyday use around the stables and for hacking out.

All three types of legwear should be reinforced where the leg lies on the saddle with strappings, either in the same material as the garment (the cheapest option) or in suede or suede-look material. Some items have an inset seat-panel made in special extra-grip fabric which increases both comfort and security in the saddle.

Legwear comes in a wide range of materials. Many of these include a degree of stretch which ensures a good fit

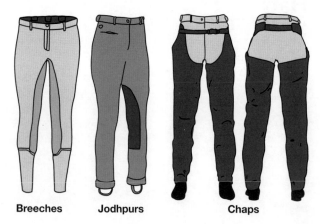

Breeches   **Jodhpurs**   **Chaps**

and allows the garment to 'give' with the rider's movements. The choice of material will be governed by individual preference, weather conditions and the type of riding you intend to do. Cost will also be a factor. As with riding boots, in winter you may wish to wear long underwear for extra warmth, in which case you must allow a little extra room under jodhpurs and breeches.

Modern legwear comes in a wide range of colours. Dark tones are especially useful for everyday wear since they do not show the dirt so much and may require less washing. For most competitive riding traditional light-coloured jodhpurs and breeches (usually fawn) are compulsory.

Another option for casual wear is a pair of hard-wearing chaps, made of hide, suede or a waterproof synthetic material. They are designed to be pulled on over jeans or trousers and fastened to a belt at the waist.

Gaiters and knee-length chaps (known as half chaps, and which fasten round the legs with straps, zips or velcro) are often worn with short boots to simulate long boots. They must be the same colour as the boots, and should not have any tassels attached. They are a less expensive and often more comfortable or practical alternative to tall riding boots.

Half chaps

Jackets

A traditional riding jacket looks smart and gives excellent protection against the weather. For ease of movement it should have one or two vents at the back. It should be free from adornments such as a velvet collar (except for the show ring), fancy buttons or a brightly coloured lining. Remember when fitting a jacket that it must allow free movement of the arms and shoulders, particularly when jumping.

1 vent

2 vents

Traditional riding jacket

Casual Coats

Quilted jackets, body warmers and other types of casual riding coat come in a wide range of styles and colours and are excellent for everyday wear. Remember, though, that bulky coats of this type are not ideal for lessons or Pony Club rallies because they make it difficult for the instructor to assess the rider's position.

Casual riding coat

Quilted bodywarmer
(or gilet)

Quilted riding jacket

Shirts

A plain shirt with a well-fitting collar is correct with a Pony Club tie. A collar-less shirt with a well-fitting neck-band is suitable with a hunting tie (also commonly known as a 'stock').

Neckwear

Pony Club Members may wear a Pony Club tie, but it should be secured with a plain bar (or Pony Club) tie slide or tie pin (see *Warning* on opposite page) to stop it from flapping about.

After the age of about 15 it is acceptable to wear a Pony Club tie or hunting tie (which should be coloured) with a tweed coat.

It is usual to wear a white hunting tie and a plain stock pin with navy blue or black coats.

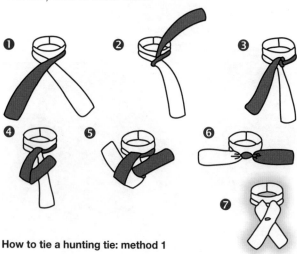

How to tie a hunting tie: method 1

WARNING
The sharp point of a tie or stock pin can cause a nasty injury to a rider during a fall or other unexpected impact. Tie slides (also known as 'clips') are therefore preferable and recommended for use whenever practicable. When stock pins are worn, they should be fixed horizontally to minimise the risk of injury as much as possible.

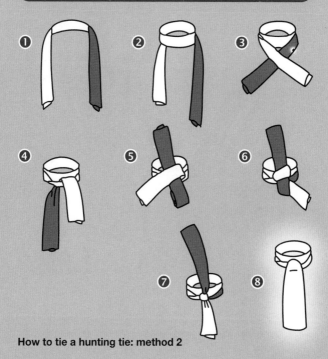

How to tie a hunting tie: method 2

Gloves

Gloves give protection against the cold and rain and provide a better grip when reins are sweaty or rain soaked. Always buy gloves that are specially designed for riding. They come in a variety of materials and styles and may have such features as pimple palm grips or other 'extra-grip' properties, reinforced rein fingers, elasticated or velcro wrist fastenings and Lycra inserts for added flexibility.

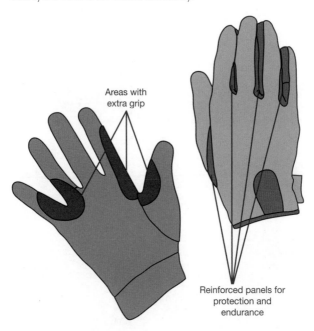

Areas with extra grip

Reinforced panels for protection and endurance

Typical riding gloves come in a variety of materials and may have 'extra-grip' and/or reinforced panels in appropriate places

The choice of glove depends very much on the use to which it will be put. For dressage schooling, for example, leather gloves are preferable as they ensure a much truer 'feel', but bear in mind that they are not suitable for use in wet weather as the reins will tend to slip through them. For other purposes, gloves may be made of cotton, string or nylon and may be lined or unlined. For everyday riding, choose gloves that wash well. **Always wear well-fitting gloves (with good grip) when lungeing, leading, loading or competing.**

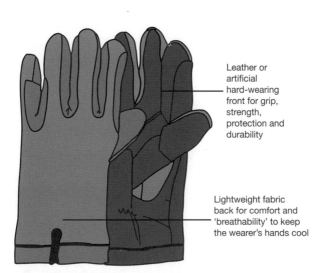

Leather or artificial hard-wearing front for grip, strength, protection and durability

Lightweight fabric back for comfort and 'breathability' to keep the wearer's hands cool

Riding gloves may feature hard-wearing fronts and lightweight backs

Underwear

Specially-designed sports underwear can be far more comfortable than conventional garments. Many riding-wear companies stock a range of suitable male and female underwear.

Waterproofs

Modern waterproofing techniques have made wet-weather wear both light and comfortable. Waxed cotton is a favourite and there are also various 'breathable' waterproof fabrics that are equally comfortable.

Waterproof coats may be short, three-quarter or full length. A long coat should be fitted with a rear vent and leg straps. Shorter ones need side vents for ease of movement. Many coats feature a cotton or fleece lining and corduroy collar for additional comfort and warmth. A storm collar, storm cuffs and pommel flap are other useful fittings for riding in wet weather.

WARNING

Be careful when riding a horse when you are wearing a full-length coat for the first time or if your horse is not used to it. The unfamilar feel of the coat may alarm him.

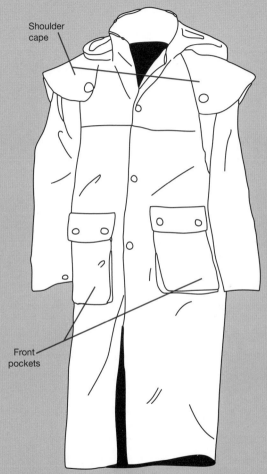

Shoulder cape

Front pockets

A full-length waterproof coat has several features which help to keep the wearer dry and comfortable

Part 2
Safety First

However well-schooled your horse or pony and however skilful you are as a rider, there is no getting away from the fact that riding is a risk sport and everyone is going to fall off at some time; and anyone who falls from a height of several feet, particularly at speed, stands a chance of injuring themselves.

Your head is one of the most vulnerable parts of your body. If you fall off, you might hit it on a fence pole or sharp stone, or you could be dragged along or kicked or trodden on by your horse. Even if you do not fall off, your head is still at risk of sharp blows from hazards such as overhanging branches. It is, therefore, irresponsible not to wear the best available protective headgear at all times when you are mounted. Remember, too, that you can be equally at risk when lungeing, long-reining or even just leading a horse, particularly a young or unpredictable one.

Bear in mind that it does not take a large, visible wound to cause brain damage. The effects of a blow that leaves only a small wound, or perhaps no visible wound at all, can be far-reaching: the real trouble may be inside the skull rather than on the outside.

To understand what happens when you bang your head, think of your brain as being rather like a lump of thick blancmange suspended in fluid in your skull and held in place by nerves, blood vessels and the spinal cord. When you fall or receive a hard blow on the head—for example from a kick—the effect is to bounce the brain against the sides of the skull or to twist it on its attachments. This is how brain damage occurs.

Hats

Riding hats are designed to minimise the risk of injury to the brain by absorbing as much of the impact of a blow as possible. The idea is to try to slow down that impact so that your brain is cushioned and therefore suffers less damage. The thick, inner layer of the hat absorbs the impact and helps to prevent the brain from moving inside the skull. The surrounding outer shell is designed to prevent sharp objects such as stones from piercing the hat.

To give maximum protection a hat needs to cover all the thin areas of the skull. Protection for the forehead and the back of the skull is particularly vital, and correct fitting of your hat is essential. If you are at all unsure, seek advice from an experienced retailer who has been trained in hat-fitting. BETA—the British Equestrian Trade Association—offers training in hat-fitting to retailers, who are then able to provide riders with a free, personalised fitting. Look for a BETA Safety Certificate displayed in the shop.

Hats and helmets come in a wide range of sizes to fit all shapes of head. A correctly-fitted one will feel comfortable and won't slip in any direction when the head is moved. Pony Club Members are advised to try several makes of hat to find the best fit. Always remember that hats are designed to be worn parallel to the ground, never on the back of the head or too low down over the forehead. All peaks—if present on a hat—should be flexible, even if they appear solid or fixed. A skull cap, for example, has no peak at all, but can be made to look smart by fitting it with a 'silk' or cover which has a soft peak.

In addition to ensuring that your hat fits correctly, it is also

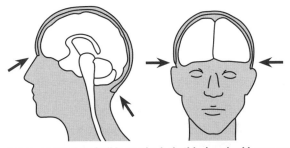

Areas where the skull is particularly thin (marked by arrows)

essential that it has a retaining harness and that you wear it fastened at all times. However well-fitting the hat, it is of no use if it slips or even falls off when you part company with your horse. A correctly-adjusted harness will keep your hat firmly in place.

Hats are constantly being improved so it is important that you keep up to date with the standards laid down in the current Pony Club rule books for your chosen sport or activity.

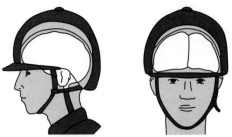

Modern riding hats are specially designed to give extra protection to the most vulnerable areas of the skull.

Pony Club Rules for Riding Hats

It is mandatory for all Members, when taking part in Pony Club activities, to wear a protective helmet manufactured to exacting safety standards.

It MUST bear the CE mark AND a quality symbol, either the BSI (British Standards Institute) Kitemark, the SAI Global symbol or the official Snell label with number. The CE symbol on its own is not sufficient to ensure consistent standard of manufacture. The PAS 015:1998 and the Snell E2001 meet higher impact criteria than other hats and therefore give more

Lightweight, rigid shell

Flexible peak

Padding inside

Fully-adjustable straps

A well-fitting riding hat is safer as well as more comfortable than a badly-fitting one. A fringe should not show at the front or hang over the ears—for safety reasons as well as aesthetic ones.

protection. Note that the prefix 'BS' on the EN 1384 standard does not mean that the hat has undergone batch testing by the BSI—the hat must contain the BSI Kitemark as well.

Hats with vertical plastic/metallic strips are permitted.

For organised endurance rides only, ventilated hats that meet one of the required standards may be worn.

Pony Club Hat Checks and Tagging

The Branch District Commissioner (DC) will appoint two Branch officials (one of whom may be the DC) who are familiar with The Pony Club's rule for hats to carry out hat checks and to tag each hat that complies with the above requirements with a Pony Club hat tag. Centre Members' hats may also be tagged by a Centre Coordinator. Once a hat has been fitted with a Pony Club tag it will not need to be checked on subsequent occasions. Tags may only be fitted by one of the two appointed Branch officials after they have personally checked the hat.

NOTE:
Tagging indicates that a hat meets the minimum standards mentioned above. No check of the fit and condition of the hat is implied. It is considered to be the responsibility of the member's parent or guardian to ensure that their hat complies with the required standards and is tagged before they go to any Pony Club event, and also to ensure that the hat manufacturer's guidelines with regard to fit and replacement are followed.

Children Under the Age of Nine

Medical advice is that children's neck muscles do not develop adequately to support a fairly heavy helmet until they are nine years of age. Therefore it may be appropriate for children under that age to wear a lightweight hat made to comply with the minimum approved standards.

HATS: DOS AND DON'TS

DO wear a correctly fitting hat at all times when mounted and when lungeing, leading, loading or long-reining a horse.

DO wear the correctly adjusted harness fastened at all times.

DO buy a new hat if your existing one receives a hard blow or if you were concussed as a result of a fall or blow. Remember that damage to the hat may not be visible and if you have another fall while wearing the same hat you may not be adequately protected.

DON'T wear your hat on the back of your head or tilted too far forward.

DON'T wear a second-hand hat—you have no way of knowing whether it has already been damaged.

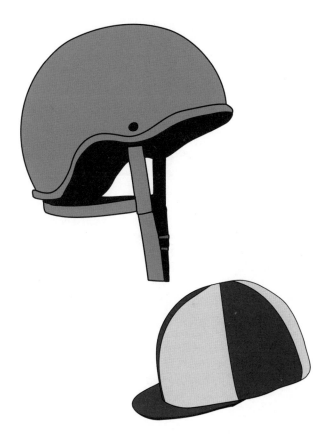

Skull caps (top)—also known as 'jockey helmets'—are the type of helmet most-frequently worn for racing and eventing. Although similar to regular riding hats, the major difference is that skull caps do not have a peak. Instead, a soft peak is a part of the optional 'silk' or helmet cover (bottom).

Body Protectors

Except for cross-country riding and pony racing (both training and competing) The Pony Club does not make the use of a body protector compulsory. However, if you ride at fast speeds or over fixed fences of any height (for example in hunter trials) you are strongly advised to wear one. Modern garments are lightweight, flexible, easy to put on and comfortable to wear. They come in a variety of styles—shop around to find one which suits your figure. As with hats, BETA trains retailers to fit body protectors correctly—look for a BETA Safety Certificate displayed in the shop.

A body protector should cover the whole circumference of the torso. At the front, the bottom edge should be not less than 25cm (9¾in) below the rib cage and should reach the level of the pelvis laterally. The top should reach the top of the sternum (breastbone).

At the back, the edge should be not less than 15cm (8in) below the level of the top of the pelvis on the average adult. The top of the garment should reach the level of the seventh cervical vertebrae (the prominent bone at the base of the neck). The armholes should be roughly circular in shape and as small as is comfortable.

In Britain, body protectors manufactured to BETA standards are recommended. Some years ago BETA brought together riding organisations, doctors, riders, manufacturers and retailers to develop the now widely recognised BETA Body Protector Standard, which meets all the requirements of the European standard. Body protectors are re-tested annually for consistency of quality of materials used and manufacture.

The BETA standard sets criteria for shock-absorption, controls the area of the body that must be covered and ensures that there are minimal gaps between the protective foam panels.

There are three levels, each designed for a different activity and carrying a colour-coded label on the protector.

- **Level 1** (black label) provides the lowest level of protection and is only considered appropriate for licensed jockeys while racing.
- **Level 2** (brown label) is suitable for low-risk situations—not including jumping, riding on the road, riding young or excitable horses or riding while inexperienced.
- **Level 3** (purple label) is considered appropriate for general riding, for competitions (including eventing) and for working with horses.

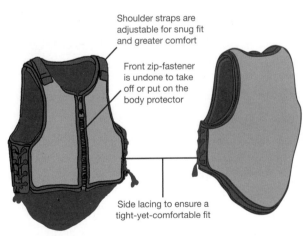

Shoulder straps are adjustable for snug fit and greater comfort

Front zip-fastener is undone to take off or put on the body protector

Side lacing to ensure a tight-yet-comfortable fit

The front and back of a typical body protector

Shoulder Protectors

There is a separate BETA standard for shoulder protectors. Research has shown that wearing shoulder protectors to BETA level 3 significantly reduces the chance of injury to the collarbone in the event of a fall.

Attached to the body protector by velcro straps

Medical card holder

Shoulder protectors are worn *in addition* to a body protector

Air Jackets

Riders who choose to wear an air jacket (which is designed to inflate in the event of a fall) must also use a normal body protector. If the rider falls, the jacket must be fully deflated or removed altogether before they are allowed to ride on. An air jacket must not be worn under a jacket. Number bibs must be fitted loosely, or with elasticated fastenings, over the air jacket.

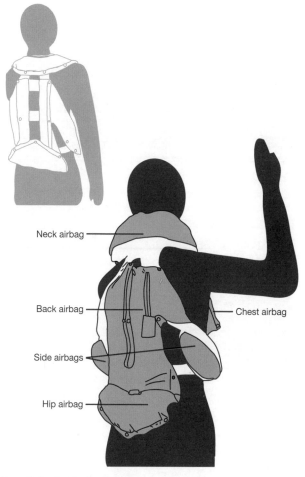

Neck airbag

Back airbag

Chest airbag

Side airbags

Hip airbag

Top: Air jacket before inflation
Below: Air jacket after inflation

BODY PROTECTOR
DOS AND DON'TS

DO replace your body protector at least every 3 to 5 years. After that time the impact-absorption properties of the foam panels may have begun to decline.

DO have your body protector checked immediately after a heavy fall. The foam should expand back to its original shape within 30 minutes. If a dent is visible, it is likely that this part of the garment has lost its impact-absorption properties. In this case, you must buy a new one.

DO take care of your body protector when it is not in use. Fasten zips and velcro fastenings and hang the garment on a clothes hanger.

DO store your body protector in a warm (not hot) place. Most garments are made from heat-sensitive foam which is why they feel increasingly comfortable as they soften and mould to your body. Keeping your protector in a warm place will ensure that it is flexible when you put it on.

DON'T use a second-hand body protector.

DON'T leave your body protector lying around at the yard or in the lorry where it can easily be damaged.

DON'T leave your body protector in a very hot car or in a damp environment.

Footwear

The safest footwear for riding is either the long leather riding boot or the jodhpur boot with elastic sides. Rubber riding boots and strong lace-up shoes with plain soles and 1.5cm (½in) heels are also acceptable, although non-leather soles do not give such good protection as leather ones. When mounted at Pony Club activities, only standard riding or jodhpur boots with a fairly smooth, thin sole and a well-defined square-cut heel may be worn. Plain black or brown half chaps or gaiters may be worn with jodhpur boots of the same colour.

The only exception to these recommendations occurs in the sport of endurance riding, when riders may need to spend time out of the saddle, running beside their horse. If heelless shoes are worn for this purpose, caged stirrups must be used (to prevent the possibility of the foot slipping through the iron).

Wellington boots, trainers and other footwear with ridged soles or with little or no heel should not be worn. Ridged soles can become caught up in the stirrups, while footwear with no clearly defined heel can slip right through the iron. Both situations are highly dangerous in the event of a fall, since the foot might become trapped in the stirrup and the rider dragged.

NOTE:
- Stirrups must be the correct size to suit the the rider's boots.
- There must be 7mm (¼in) clearance on either side between the boot and the stirrup iron.
- There is a tendency for manufacturers to put treaded soles on riding boots. These may significantly increase the risk of the foot becoming trapped in the stirrup in the event of a fall, which could result in serious injury.
- Boots and stirrups with interlocking treads are not permitted, nor are the boots or treads individually.

Spectacles and Contact Lenses

There is an element of danger in riding in spectacles, but many people do so all their lives without suffering injury. Ideally, those with defective vision should wear contact lenses. If you can't wear them, take advice from your optician on the safest type of spectacle frames and lenses.

Jewellery

Jewellery, except for a plain tie pin or—preferably—a tie slide, should never be worn when riding. Earrings, however small, are particularly dangerous. They can become caught on overhanging twigs, in your jacket collar, or the chinstrap of your hat, and cause nasty injuries to your ears. Nose-studs/ rings are just as dangerous.

Tie slides are preferable to tie pins for safety reasons (*see* page 16), but if a tie pin is worn it should be fixed horizontally, and **never** vertically, because of the danger of injury to your chest or chin if knocked downwards or upwards.

WARNING

Pony Club Members contemplating having their ears (or any other part of the body) pierced should be aware that they will not be allowed to compete until such time as the 'sleepers' can safely be removed. Sleepers have in the past caused injuries following falls. There are vulnerable blood vessels behind the ear, and if a facial nerve is pierced partial paralysis of the face can occur.

Hair

Long hair should always be tied back or plaited and put up when working around horses. If it is not, there is a risk of it becoming caught up or of frightening a horse if it suddenly flaps in his face.

When wearing a riding hat, a fringe should not show at the front or at the sides for both safety and aestheic reasons.

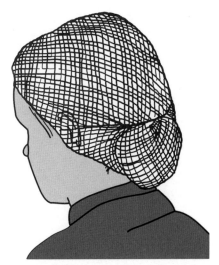

Long hair should be plaited, secured with a dark-coloured elastic band, twisted into a bun, and covered with a hairnet before the riding hat is put on.

Riding on the Road

Horses and riders are especially vulnerable on the road due to some motorists' lack of consideration for horses and the high speeds of too many vehicles. Riding in bright daylight is dangerous enough, but when light conditions are poor then it becomes doubly so. It is not always possible to avoid riding on the road but there is no excuse for not making yourself and your horse as conspicuous as possible, whatever the time of day and whatever the light conditions.

A wide range of high visibility clothing for horse and rider is now available. Made of fluorescent, brightly-coloured materials, its purpose is to make the wearers visible to other road users at long distances. It is particularly useful in dangerous situations, such as narrow lanes and on bends. Research suggests that high visibility clothing enables drivers to spot a horse and rider some three seconds sooner than they would otherwise do.

Most items come in yellow, although bright pink is also an option. For riding in less-bright conditions your 'hi-vis' equipment should be fitted with strips of reflective material. These strips appear grey in daylight but they give brilliant reflection of light in gloomy conditions.

Choosing the best 'hi-vis' equipment is not always easy since it is hard to judge the reflectivity of an item in a shop. Also, without some form of guarantee, riders cannot know how well a garment will retain its colour and reflectivity when washed. To help riders make the safest choices, BETA operates a High Visibility Certification Scheme. When asked by the manufacturers, the Association will carry out checks on their high visibility items. Then, if they come up

Yellow tabard or jacket fitted with a broad reflective strip or strips, preferably encircling the whole body. A tabard or jacket can also be inscribed with a warning message such as 'Pass Wide and Slow' but bear in mind that if there are too many words drivers may be tempted to approach too close for comfort in order to read them. A large 'L' for learner is a good alternative for novice riders and for riders on young horses.

OR

Yellow body warmer fitted with reflective strips

OR

Yellow Sam Browne belt with reflective strips plus yellow arm and leg bands fitted with reflective strips

Yellow hat-cover with a reflective band

Yellow exercise sheet with reflective strips

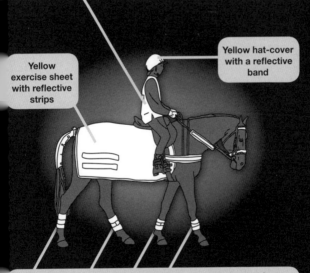

Reflective leg bands can be fitted over brushing or tendon boots or, in some cases, directly on to the legs. The movement of the horse's legs makes these particularly effective.

to standard, they award them one of three colour-coded certification marks. These indicate the suitability of a garment for a particular purpose.

The certification mark assures riders that garments and accessories conform to one of the three high-visibility standards for equestrian clothing. Those included in the scheme can be identified by the colour coded sewn-in labels, swing tags or stickers.

- **EN471** is represented by an aqua-coloured label. This is suitable for professional use, such as by grooms exercising horses out on the roads.
- **EN1150** is represented by a royal blue label. This is suitable for non-professional use by leisure riders.
- **EN13356** is represented by a navy blue label. This is suitable for high visibility accessories, including detachable belts and arm and hat bands.

There is wide range of high visibility items to choose from. As well as the commonly seen hat bands, tabards and Sam Browne belts, riders can buy 'hi-vis' gloves and glove covers, arm and leg bands, stirrup reflectors and leg lights.

Equipment for the horse includes leg bands, used either fitted over protective boots or directly on the leg; noseband, rein, browband and martingale bands; tailguards, and an eye-catching horse bib, which goes around the neck and fastens to the D rings on the saddle. Whatever you choose, it makes sense for you and your horse to wear as much reflective equipment as possible when riding on the road.

The Law and Riding on the Road

In Britain the law requires that when riding on the road, children under the age of 14 **must** wear an approved safety helmet, securely fastened. The Pony Club strongly recommends the wearing of safely helmets specifically designed for horse riding by all riders regardless of age.

On the Ground

It is important to wear sensible clothes when working with horses on the ground as well as when riding. Horses and ponies are big, strong animals who require skilful training and careful handling. Even then they can still be unpredictable and given to making sudden movements which can take the most experienced of horsemen by surprise. The ability to move out of the way quickly has saved many a handler from being leaned on, bitten, trodden on, kicked or otherwise hurt by an unexpected lapse of good manners on the part of their equine friend.

Clothes for Stable Work

Neat, well-fitting (but not too tight) clothing is easier to move around in than loose, flapping garments, which can so easily become caught up on 'foreign objects' such as the bolt of a door or the handle of a wheel barrow.

Depending on the weather, a shirt, sweatshirt or sweater is ideal for work around the stables. If it is cold enough to wear a body warmer or jacket, you should keep it fastened. A flapping coat can easily become caught up and might even distract or frighten a nervous horse. It also looks untidy and unworkmanlike. The same applies to long, flapping hair.

In very hot weather there is always the temptation to wear flimsy, sleeveless t-shirts or sun-tops. Be warned! If a horse unexpectedly swings his head round to bite—and he may well do so if he is being irritated by flies or is simply ticklish when being groomed—his teeth can make very painful contact with a bare upper arm or shoulder. If you are wearing a shirt with sleeves, even short ones, there is at least a chance that his teeth will grab only the material rather than your skin.

Comfortable jeans, trousers or jodhpurs (dark coloured ones are the most practical) are all suitable for stable work. Again they should fit well, without being so tight that they make bending down difficult.

Neat, comfortable and well-fitting garments are safest and most comfortable for stable work

Footwear for Stable Work

When mucking out, particularly in wet weather, there is probably nothing to beat Wellington (or 'welly') boots. They are waterproof and easily washed clean, and the soles give good grip under most conditions. On the minus side, they tend to make your feet cold, though this problem can be largely overcome by choosing a boot half a size bigger than your feet and wearing walking-boot or other thick socks. Alternatively, choose boots made of neoprene, which are much warmer to wear. The main problem associated with all 'rubber' boots is that they do not give much protection should your horse inadvertently step on to your foot.

Sturdy short boots will give more protection, and they do enable you to move quickly when necessary.

Jodhpur and leather riding boots probably give the best protection to your feet, but you may not wish to make them dirty when mucking out or grooming.

Lungeing and Long-Reining

Always wear comfortable, well-fitting clothes and comfortable boots when lungeing or long-reining. Gloves are also essential—they give extra grip on the rein(s) and prevent rope-burns should the horse suddenly pull away from you. Always wear a hard hat, too, with the chin strap correctly adjusted and fastened.

Leading a Horse

Many people lead horses about with no thought to their own safety: with one hand on the headcollar, or gripping a piece of string, perhaps, or in clothes in which they could not possibly move quickly should the need arise. In most cases horses do behave perfectly well and no harm is done. But accidents can happen, even with the calmest animal. If there is any possibility of a led horse being frightened by something unfamiliar, or if you are simply unfamiliar with him, then take sensible precautions. **Wear gloves. Wear a hard hat** in case he rears up and strikes out. **Wear boots** to protect your feet should he jump around. He should, of course, be led on a suitable lead rein or rope. Young horses, in particular, are unpredictable, so **be prepared.**

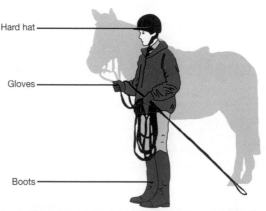

Hard hat ——

Gloves ——

Boots ——

When lungeing, long-reining, loading or leading a horse, it is important to wear clothes which protect you from the inherent dangers.

<u>SAFETY CHECKLIST</u>

ALWAYS wear a hard hat and gloves when lungeing or long-reining, and also when leading a young horse or one with whom you are not familiar.

ALWAYS wear comfortable, well-fitting clothes and footwear that allow you complete freedom of movement.

NEVER wear sandals or other flimsy shoes when working with horses.

DON'T wear skimpy, sleeveless tops.

DON'T wear baggy, flapping clothes.

DON'T wear jewellery.

45

Part 3
Leisure Riding

While organised equestrian sports have their own rules governing participants' dress, the individual rider is, of course, free to wear whatever he or she chooses when taking part in non-competitive activities such as schooling, hacking out and so on. When riding on the roads—with all the potential dangers that it involves—the only legal requirement concerns children under the age of 14 who must wear an approved safely helmet.

The onus is therefore on the individual to behave in a responsible manner when deciding what to wear for everyday leisure riding. By taking sensible precautions you will not only guard against injury but you could also save other people a good deal of trouble.

Whether you are schooling, doing road work or perhaps enjoying a trekking holiday, as always there are two golden rules governing the rider's equipment: it must be safe, to protect you from injury, and it should be comfortable, to enable you to ride to the best of your ability.

Schooling at Home and Off-road Hacking

Sweaters, sweatshirts, casual riding coats, trousers, jodhpurs, breeches and chaps are fine, provided you also wear safe footwear and a correctly-fitted hat with the harness fastened at all times when you are mounted.

When schooling over cross country fences it is sensible to take the same precautions that you would when competing: i.e. wear a body protector (see pages 30–32).

Riding on the Roads

For detailed recommendations regarding safety equipment for both you and your horse, see pages 38–41.

Riding at a School

No riding establishment worth attending will allow anyone to ride without a correctly-fitted hat and safe footwear. Some schools keep a supply of hats of various sizes, which may be borrowed by beginners who do not already have their own. However, a borrowed hat will never fit as well as one fitted to your particular head by a trained person. If you intend to ride regularly, you should buy your own as soon as possible.

Riding Holidays

When booking a non-instructional riding holiday (trekking, post-trekking, day rides, etc), ask the centre's advice regarding appropriate dress and particular equipment that you may need.

LEISURE RIDING DOS AND DON'TS

DO wear a correctly-fitted hat, with the harness fastened, at all times when you are mounted.

DO wear safe footwear at all times, both when you are mounted and when you are moving around horses and ponies while you are on the ground.

DO wear a body protector if you plan to jump cross country fences—particularly when you are schooling a young horse.

DO wear comfortable, well-fitting clothes specially designed for riding. If you are uncomfortable, you will not ride to the best of your ability, nor will you be able to concentrate one hundred per cent on what you are doing.

DON'T wear jewellery. Earrings, studs, necklaces and rings can all become caught up and cause painful injuries.

DON'T leave long hair flapping loose. It, too, can easily become caught up and can distract or scare a horse.

DON'T wear your coat unfastened. It looks sloppy, and a flapping coat can distract or scare a horse.

DON'T ride on the road without rider and horse both wearing suitable high-visibility clothing.

Part 4
Pony Club Activities and Sports

The rules of The Pony Club require all Members to be neatly turned out at all times and to wear correct protective clothing whenever they are mounted. New clothes are not expected, but what is worn should be clean and tidy.

Protective headgear, made to the recommended standard, correctly fitted and worn with the chin-strap fastened, is compulsory for all Pony Club activities, competitive or otherwise. This rule on hats also applies to all mounted prize-giving ceremonies.

Jodhpur boots or long riding boots are also compulsory. Trainers, Wellingtons and other similar footwear are not permitted for riding. Jeans are not recommended because they can cause chafing. Half-chaps may be worn at rallies and in some competitions. They should match the colour of the rider's boots and be of a plain design, with no tassels.

The wearing of earrings, nose studs and other jewellery is not permitted and may incur elimination from competitions.

At competitive events, while walking the course or when dismounted in the collecting ring, riders must be tidily dressed, though not necessarily in riding clothes.

Working Rallies

Items of dress which are correct for boys and girls at working rallies and for Associates when instructing are illustrated here.

NOTE:
- Some Branches allow Branch polo shirts and sweatshirts to be worn for rallies, depending on the weather.
- Half chaps or gaiters are allowed. They should be plain black or brown to match the colour of the boots. Tassels are not allowed.
- Boots and stirrups with interlocking treads are not permitted, nor are the boots or treads individually.

> **Jodhpurs *OR* breeches**
> (fawn or cream,
> NOT white or dark colours)

> **Jodhpur boots** (black or brown)
> *OR* **long riding boots**

Protective **hat** manufactured to one of the minimum approved standards, with a dark blue or black cover. Hats with vertical plastic/metallic strips are permitted. All hats must be fitted with a Pony Club tag.

Shirt with collar and **tie**

Sweater *OR* v-necked pullover (without jacket if weather permits)

Riding jacket

Protective **hat**, manufactured to one of the minimum approved standards, with a dark blue or black **cover**. Hats with vertical plastic/metallic strips are permitted. All hats must be fitted with a Pony Club tag.

Pony Club tie

White **shirt** with long sleeves (which should not be rolled up)

Jodhpur boots (black or brown) *OR* long **riding boots**. Boots must have a fairly thin sole and a well-defined, square-cut heel.

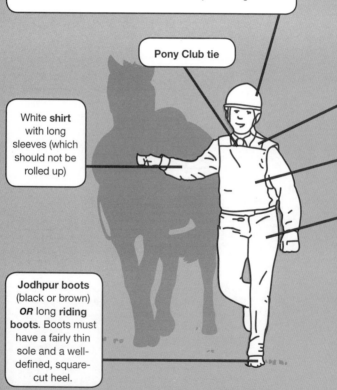

54

Mounted Games

Items of dress which are correct for boys and girls when taking part in mounted games are illustrated here.

White **sweatshirt** and/or colourless transparent or white **waterproof garment** with long sleeves, which may be worn over the shirt in cold or wet weather.

Bib with Branch or team colours as appropriate. (Bibs are worn over shirts or sweatshirts.)

Jodhpurs (fawn or cream, NOT white or dark colours)

NOTE:
- Half chaps or gaiters are allowed. They should be plain black or brown to match the colour of the boots. Tassels are not allowed.
- Boots and stirrups with interlocking treads are not permitted, nor are the boots or treads individually.
- The reserve rider, when taking part unmounted, must also wear a hat.
- Badges are optional. If worn, they should be of cloth, not metal, and may be sewn on to the bib.
- Long hair should be secured appropriately.
- Jewellery and wristwatches may not be worn.
- Spurs are not allowed.
- Electronic devices (headphones, mobile phones, etc., enabling another person to communicate with the rider) are not allowed while the rider is competing.

Dressage

The Pony Club expects competitors to wear plain dress. Clothes should be clean, neat and tidy. While dismounted in the collecting area, competitors must be tidily dressed, but not necessarily in riding clothes. At prize-giving ceremonies, whether mounted or unmounted, competitors must be correctly dressed in their competition riding clothes. The items illustrated here are correct for boys and girls competing in dressage.

NOTE:

- Half chaps or gaiters are allowed. They should be plain black or brown to match the colour of the boots. Tassels are not allowed.
- Boots and stirrups with interlocking treads are not permitted, nor are the boots or treads individually.
- Spurs may only be worn by full B Test holders or with the permission of the District Commissioner or Centre Proprietor. Members without the B Test should carry proof of this permission. Spurs must be blunt, without rowels or sharp edges. If they are curved, the curve must be downwards and the shank must point straight to the back and not exceed 3cm in length. Spurs that have a smooth rotating ball on the shank are permitted.
- If a competitor's chinstrap comes undone during a test, the rider may, without penalty, stop to re-fasten it. If a competitor's hat comes off during a test, the rider must dismount to recover the hat, or have it passed up from the ground. Again, no penalty is imposed.
- Long hair should be secured appropriately.
- No jewellery may be worn apart from a Pony Club badge, a stock pin or tie slide **worn horizontally**, and a wristwatch.
- Floral button-holes and brightly coloured accessories should not be worn.
- A whip of any length may be carried during the test (including at Area competitions and the Championships). It may be carried in either hand, but must be in the rein hand when saluting. If, in the opinion of the judge, the whip is misused, the rider will be eliminated. If the whip is dropped during a test, it may not be picked up.

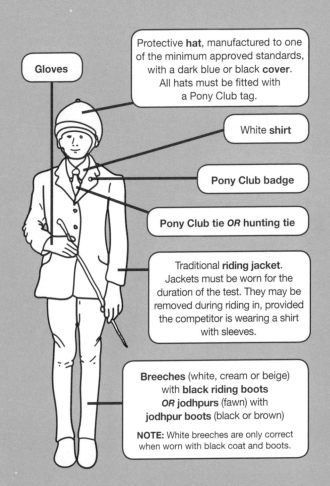

Gloves

Protective **hat**, manufactured to one of the minimum approved standards, with a dark blue or black **cover**. All hats must be fitted with a Pony Club tag.

White **shirt**

Pony Club badge

Pony Club tie *OR* **hunting tie**

Traditional **riding jacket**. Jackets must be worn for the duration of the test. They may be removed during riding in, provided the competitor is wearing a shirt with sleeves.

Breeches (white, cream or beige) with **black riding boots** *OR* **jodhpurs** (fawn) with **jodhpur boots** (black or brown)

NOTE: White breeches are only correct when worn with black coat and boots.

Protective **hat**, manufactured to one of the minimum approved standards, with a dark blue or black **cover**. Hats with vertical plastic/metallic strips are permitted. All hats must be fitted with a Pony Club tag. A hat must be worn at all times while the rider is mounted, including at prize-giving ceremonies. The chinstrap must be fastened at all times. For organized endurance rides only, **ventilated hats** that meet one of the required standards may be worn.

Shirt *OR* jersey. A lightweight shirt with long sleeves and a collar is recommended.

Breeches *OR* jodhpurs, plain or coloured

Standard **riding boots *OR* jodhpur boots** with a fairly smooth, thin sole and a well-defined, square-cut heel

Endurance Riding

Dress for endurance riding is less formal than for other equestrian sports. At the lower levels conventional long riding boots with breeches may be perfectly comfortable. However, during longer rides most competitors spend some time running beside their horses to give them a breather. In these circumstances footwear with cushioned soles and good ankle support is preferable. Half-chaps are popular, as are close-fitting riding 'tights' with added padding in strategic places. Comfortable underwear is also essential for longer rides and the present-day range of specially-designed pants and tops are ideal for endurance riders.

The Pony Club expects endurance riders to wear suitable and safe dress. New equipment is not expected, but what is worn must be clean, neat and tidy.

The items illustrated here are correct for endurance riding.

NOTE:
- Body protectors are optional. It is recommended that a rider's body protector should not be more than 2% of the rider's body weight.
- If an air jacket is used, it must not be worn under any other item of clothing. Number bibs should be fitted loosely or with elasticated fastenings over air jackets.
- Heelless shoes may be worn but if they are, caged stirrups are compulsory.
- Boots and stirrups with interlocking treads are not permitted, nor are the boots or treads individually.
- Long hair should be secured appropriately.
- Riders are advised to wear a wristwatch and to carry a mobile phone.
- No jewellery is permitted other than a wedding ring, or a tie slide or tie pin worn horizontally.
- Spurs are not permitted.
- No rider may carry, use or permit to be used a whip greater than 75cm (30in) in length.

Polo

Polo is a fast contact sport and can therefore be dangerous. As well as the usual safety equipment riders are urged to wear additional items such as goggles and gum shields.

The items shown are correct for polo players at tournaments.

> **Team shirt** with number on the back to indicate position of player

> **Breeches _OR_ jeans** (white). At the lower levels, players may wear jodhpurs with half chaps.

NOTE:
- Boots and stirrups with interlocking treads are not permitted, nor are the boots or treads individually.
- Wearing face guards/goggles and gum shields is recommended. Gum shields should be properly fitted by a dentist.
- Long hair should be secured appropriately.
- Jewellery and studs must not be worn.
- Spurs may be worn except by riders at the three lower levels. They must be blunt and may not exceed 3cm in length. If they are curved, the curve must be downward and the shank must point straight to the back.
- Whips may not exceed 122cm (48in) total length, including the tag. Broken whips are not allowed.
- Electronic devices (headphones, mobile phones, etc.), enabling another person to communicate with the rider, are not allowed while the rider is competing.

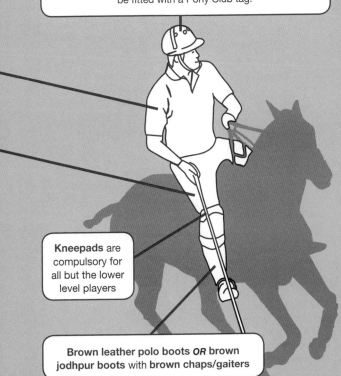

Protective **polo helmet** manufactured to one of the minimum approved standards. HX and JOR players may instead wear a jockey skull or other style of riding hat which, again, must be manufactured to one of the minimum approved standards. A protective helmet/hat is mandatory. All helmets/hats must be fitted with a Pony Club tag.

Kneepads are compulsory for all but the lower level players

Brown leather polo boots OR brown jodhpur boots with **brown chaps/gaiters**

For dressage and showjumping, a **shirt** with collar and Pony Club **tie** with **stock pin** *OR* collarless **shirt** with white or cream **hunting tie**. A traditional **riding jacket** must be worn with a Pony Club **tie** or **hunting tie**. Jackets may be removed during riding in, provided the competitor is wearing a shirt with sleeves.

A protective **hat**, manufactured to one of the minimum approved standards, is mandatory in all three phases of eventing. It is strongly recommended that a jockey skull cap plus silk is worn for all cross-country riding. When riding over fences 0.80m (2ft 7½in) high and above, in tests, rallies or training, a jockey skull cap is mandatory.

For cross country, a **shirt** and **tie** or secured **hunting tie** with **sweater** are recommended. Long sleeves are compulsory (to protect the rider's arms from serious grazing injuries). **Stock pins** should be removed.

Breeches (beige or white) *OR* **jodhpurs** (beige)

Riding boots *OR* **jodhpur boots** with a fairly smooth, thin sole and well-defined square-cut heel.

Eventing

The Pony Club expects competitors to wear plain dress. Apart from cross country colours and silks, brightly coloured accessories must not be worn. The items illustrated here are correct for eventing.

A **body protector** may be worn for dressage, is recommended for showjumping and is compulsory for cross country. It is strongly advised that the body protector should not impede flexibility or balance. It is recommended that a body protector should not be more than 2% of the rider's weight. Riders who choose to use the 'Woof Wear Exo' body cage must lodge a key with the event organizer when they collect their number.

If an **air jacket** is worn, it must only be used in addition to a normal body protector. In the event of a fall, it must be fully deflated or removed before the rider continues. An air jacket must not be worn under any item of clothing. Number bibs should be fitted loosely or with elasticated fastenings over air jackets.

A **medical armband** is compulsory for cross country but recommended at all times. It should be worn on the arm or the shoulder protector/pad of the body protector.

Gloves are compulsory for the dressage test and optional for cross country and showjumping.

EVENTING NOTE:

- Spurs may only be worn by full B Test holders or with the permission of the District Commissioner or Centre Proprietor. Members without the B Test should carry proof of this permission. Spurs must be blunt, without rowels or sharp edges. If they are curved, the curve must be downwards and the shank must point straight to the back and must not exceed 3cm in length. Spurs with a smooth rotating ball on the shank are permitted. Sharp spurs may not be worn.

- A white hunting tie should be worn with a black or blue coat, and a tie or coloured hunting tie with a tweed hacking jacket. The Pony Club coloured hunting tie may be worn with any jacket.

- Half chaps or gaiters are allowed. They should be plain black or brown to match the colour of the boots. Tassels are not allowed.

- Other than a wristwatch, wedding ring, a stock pin worn horizontally or a tie slide, no jewellery is permitted. It is recommended that stock pins are removed for cross country.

- Button-holes should not be worn.

- In the collecting ring and while course walking (both cross country and showjumping) competitors must be tidily dressed but not necessarily in riding clothes. However, competitors should be dressed in their riding clothes when walking the showjumping course at the Championships after 9 a.m. on the day of the competition.

- At prize-giving ceremonies competitors must be correctly dressed in their competition riding clothes whether they are mounted or dismounted.

- In dressage a whip of any length may be carried at Levels 1–3. No whips are allowed at Levels 4 and 5. In showjumping no rider may carry a whip greater than 75cm (30in) or less than 45cm (18in) in length overall. In cross country no rider may carry or use a whip that is weighted at the end or exceeds 75cm in length.

- Watches which have the ability to record time with a stop/start button are not allowed at all Pony Club one-day events and up to BE100.

- Electronic devices (headphones, mobile phones, etc.), enabling another person to communicate with the rider, are not allowed while the rider is competing.

Hunter Trials

There is no governing body for the sport of Hunter Trials, and so there are no binding rules regarding dress. Traditionally, riders wore a tweed coat, a shirt with a hunting tie, breeches and hunting boots or jodhpurs and jodhpur boots. Nowadays, many riders sensibly wear a body protector, which is more comfortable when worn with cross country clothes than with a jacket.

The following items are recommended for Members of The Pony Club:

- **Protective hat**, manufactured to one of the minimum approved standards, with a dark blue or black cover. All hats must be fitted with a Pony Club tag.
- **Body protector**.
- **Tweed jacket**.
- **Shirt** with collar, and tie with plain bar tie slide.
- **Jodhpurs** (fawn) with **jodhpur boots**
  OR breeches (fawn) with **riding boots**.

OR

- Long-sleeved **shirt** or **sweater** with **hunting tie**.
- **Body protector**.
- **Jodhpurs** (fawn) with jodhpur boots.
  OR breeches (fawn) with riding boots.
- **Gloves**.

NOTE:
- Blunt spurs may be worn if required.

A protective **hat** manufactured to one of the minimum approved standards is mandatory. Riders are advised to wear the hat that is considered to provide the best protection. Hats with ventilation holes or slits are discouraged (due to the likelihood of penetration by a sharp object). Hats with titanium strips and peaks are not recommended. Riders must wear a hat, with the chin strap fastened, at all times when mounted, including at prize-giving ceremonies. All hats must be fitted with a Pony Club tag.

Breeches, light-coloured **jodhpurs**, white **riding trousers** *OR* white **jeans**

Riding boots *OR* **jodhpur boots** with a smooth, fairly thin sole and a well-defined, square-cut heel

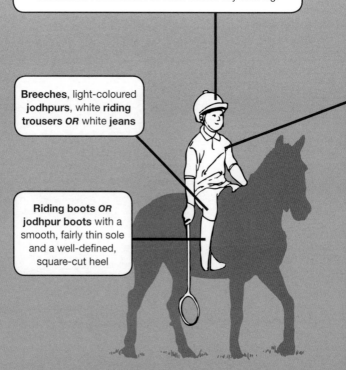

Polocrosse

Like polo, polocrosse is a fast game and because it involves the use of a stick it is potentially dangerous. Riders are advised to wear extra protection, particularly for the face.

The items illustrated here are correct for polocrosse players.

Team shirt with number to indicate position of player *OR* a shirt plus numbered **tabard**

NOTE:
- Half chaps or gaiters are allowed. They should be plain black or brown to match the colour of the boots. Tassels are not allowed.
- Knee pads may be worn (brown, black, cream or white). They must be made of soft fabric or leather and must be pliable.
- Players may not wear buckles or studs on the upper part of their boots or knee pads in such a way that they could cause damage to another player's boots or breeches.
- The wearing of face guards is recommended. If worn they must be fitted to a Pony Club approved hat (AS/NZS 3838 is the only approved hat suitable for fitting a face guard).
- Jewellery and studs must not be worn.
- Boots and stirrups with interlocking treads are not permitted, nor are the boots or treads individually.
- Spurs may only be used with the written permission of the DC or the Centre Proprietor. If worn they must be blunt and made of metal. Rowels or sharp edges are not permitted. If the spurs are curved, the curve must be downwards. The shank must point straight to the back and be not more than 3cm long. Sharp spurs may not be worn.

Racing

Pony Club race days provide an opportunity for all Branches interested in racing to compete against each other and to encourage a high standard of riding. As a high-speed sport, it is essential that riders wear suitable safety gear. All riders are required to wear the items illustrated here.

> **Body protector** (compulsory). Riders who choose to use the Woof Wear Body Cage EXO must lodge a key with the event organizer when they collect their number. If an air jacket is worn, it must only be used in addition to a normal body protector. In the event of a fall, it must be fully deflated or removed before the rider continues. **An air jacket must not be worn under *any* item of clothing.** Number bibs should be fitted loosely or with elasticated fastenings over the air jacket.

NOTE:
- Half chaps are allowed. They should be plain black or brown to match the colour of the boots. Tassels are not allowed.
- Stirrups should be of the correct size to suit the rider's boots. There must be 7mm (¼in) clearance on either side between the boot and the stirrup iron.
- **Riders must wear their medical armbands at all times when mounted, with the correct card enclosed.**
- Spurs and whips are not allowed.
- Wristwatches and jewellery may not be worn.
- Goggles may be worn.

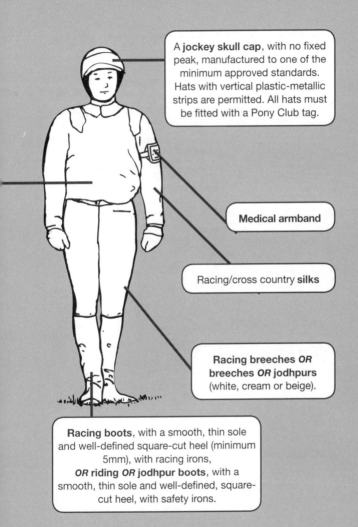

A **jockey skull cap**, with no fixed peak, manufactured to one of the minimum approved standards. Hats with vertical plastic-metallic strips are permitted. All hats must be fitted with a Pony Club tag.

Medical armband

Racing/cross country **silks**

Racing breeches OR breeches OR jodhpurs (white, cream or beige).

Racing boots, with a smooth, thin sole and well-defined square-cut heel (minimum 5mm), with racing irons, **OR** riding **OR** jodhpur boots, with a smooth, thin sole and well-defined, square-cut heel, with safety irons.

Protective **hat**, manufactured to one of the minimum approved standards, with a dark blue or black cover. Hats with vertical plastic/metallic strips are permitted. All hats must be fitted with a Pony Club tag.

Pony Club tie with **tie slide**

Shirt with collar

Traditional **riding jacket**

Breeches (white, cream or beige) with black **riding boots** *OR* **jodhpurs** (fawn) with **jodhpur boots** (black or brown)

70

Showjumping

All riders are required to wear the items illustrated.

NOTE:
- Half chaps and gaiters are allowed. They should be plain black or brown to match the colour of the boots. Tassels are not allowed.
- Boots and stirrups with interlocking treads are not permitted, nor are the boots or treads individually.
- Neither the feet nor the stirrup leathers or irons may be attached to the girth, nor the feet attached to the stirrup irons.
- Long hair should be secured appropriately.
- Other than a wristwatch, wedding ring, a tie pin worn horizontally or a tie slide, no jewellery is permitted.
- Button-holes should not be worn.
- While walking the course and when dismounted in the collecting ring, competitors must be tidily dressed but not necessarily in riding clothes.
- At prize-giving ceremonies, whether mounted or dismounted, competitors must be correctly dressed in their competition riding clothes.
- Spurs may only be worn by full B Test holders or with the permission of the District Commissioner or Centre Proprietor. Members without the B Test should carry proof of this permission. Spurs must be blunt, without rowels or sharp edges. If they are curved, the curve must be downwards and the shank must point straight to the back and must not exceed 3cm in length. Spurs with a smooth rotating ball on the shank are permitted. Sharp spurs may not be worn.
- No rider may carry, use or permit to be used a whip greater than 75cm (30in) or less than 45cm (17¾in) in length overall.
- Electronic devices (headphones, mobile phones, etc., enabling another person to communicate with the rider) are not allowed while the rider is competing.
- Body protectors are optional. It is recommended that a rider's body protector should not be more than 2% of the rider's body weight.

Tetrathlon

The tetrathlon, consisting of riding, running, shooting and swimming, is the only Pony Club sport in which girls and boys compete separately. The riding phase is normally a cross country course, so riders should wear the same as they would for the cross country phase of eventing. However, in some circumstances—for instance if the ground is unsuitable for cross country—the riding phase may take the form of a showjumping course.

The items illustrated here are correct for both girls and boys.

> **Shirt** with collar and **Pony Club tie** *OR* collarless **shirt** with coloured **hunting tie** worn with a **hacking jacket** *OR* **cross country colours**

> A **medical armband** is compulsory for all levels of cross country

> **Breeches** (white, cream or beige) *OR* **jodhpurs** (fawn)

> **Riding boots** *OR* **jodhpur boots** with a fairly smooth, thin sole and well-defined square-cut heel

A protective **hat**, manufactured to one of the approved minimum standards, is mandatory. It is strongly recommended that a jockey skull cap with no fixed peak is worn for all cross-country riding. When riding over fences 0.80m high and above, a jockey skull cap is mandatory. All hats must be fitted with a Pony Club tag.

A **body protector** is compulsory for cross-country riding. It is recommended that a rider's body protector should not be more than 2% of their body weight. Riders who choose to use the Woof Wear Body Cage EXO must lodge a key with the event organizer when they collect their number. If an air jacket is worn, it must only be used in addition to a normal body protector. In the event of a fall, it must be fully deflated or removed before the rider continues. An air jacket must not be worn under any item of clothing. Number bibs should be fitted loosely or with elasticated fastenings over air jackets.

73

TETRATHLON NOTE:
- Half chaps are allowed. They should be plain black or brown to match the colour of the boots. Tassels are not allowed.
- Boots and stirrups with interlocking treads are not permitted, nor are the boots or treads individually.
- Other than a wedding ring, no jewellery is permitted. It is recommended that stock pins are removed for cross country.
- Long hair should be secured appropriately.
- Spurs may only be worn by full B Test holders or with the permission of the District Commissioner or Centre Proprietor. Members without the B Test should carry proof of this permission. Spurs must be blunt, without rowels or sharp edges. If they are curved, the curve must be downwards and the shank must point straight to the back and must not exceed 3cm in length. Spurs with a smooth rotating ball on the shank are permitted. Sharp spurs may not be worn.
- No rider may carry, use or permit to be used a whip exceeding 76.2cm (30in) in length overall.
- Electronic devices (headphones, mobile phones, etc.), enabling another person to communicate with the rider, are not allowed while the rider is competing.
- Body protectors are optional. It is recommended that a rider's body protector should not be more than 2% of the rider's body weight.

Protective **hat**, manufactured to one of the minimum approved standards, with a dark blue or black cover.

Shirt with collar, and **Pony Club tie** with **tie slide**
OR
collar-less shirt with **Pony Club hunting tie** and **stock pin**

Hunting

There are no mandatory rules for what to wear when riding to hounds, but the dress adopted by the different categories of rider at various times of year does follow a well-defined pattern. Generally speaking, hunting clothes are designed for comfort, to keep the wearer warm and dry, to give protection from the inevitable knocks received when riding across country, and to look neat and tidy.

The items illustrated here are correct for Pony Club Members.

NOTE:
- Riders may carry a hunting whip with thong and lash or short stick with a hunting-whip handle but no thong.
- Spurs may be worn if necessary.
- A body protector is optional and should be worn under a jacket.

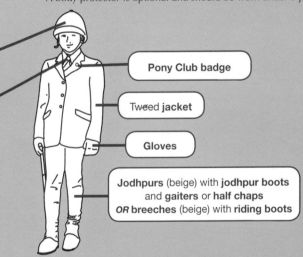

Pony Club badge

Tweed jacket

Gloves

Jodhpurs (beige) with **jodhpur boots** and **gaiters** or **half chaps**
OR **breeches** (beige) with **riding boots**

Part 5
Other
Activities

Showing

The overall aim in showing classes is for the rider to complement the pony or horse rather than to detract from it. Therefore bright colours (including coat linings), large buttonholes and jewellery should be avoided.

When tying on your number, always use a cord or ribbon of the same colour as your coat. This looks much neater than the ribbon (usually light coloured) supplied with the number.

Hair should be neat and tidy, **with no fringe showing at the front**. Girls' hair ribbons should be kept to a minimum and bright colours should be avoided.

As in other equestrian sports, safe headgear is more commonly seen in the show ring than in the past. In the jumping phase of working hunter classes a hat manufactured to one of the current minimum standards must be worn.

With the exception of certain rules governing hats, whips and spurs, there are few mandatory requirements in the showing world, although it is customary to follow the guidelines given in the following pages. If you are in any doubt as to what to wear for a particular class, consult the society or association under whose rules the class or show is being judged. Or watch the experts—they usually get it right.

The items of dress mentioned in the following pages are customary in the various children's showing classes.

Show Ponies

PAS 015 or EN 1384 **skull cap/ riding hat**, correctly secured, with dark blue or black cover)

A small **buttonhole** may be worn

Shirt with collar, and **tie** with plain bar **tie slide**

Dark blue or brown **coat**

Gloves (leather or string)

Jodhpurs (cream or fawn)

Plain or leather-covered **show cane**

Jodhpur boots (brown)

Show Ponies Side-Saddle

- PAS 015 or EN 1384 **skull cap/riding hat**, correctly secured, with dark blue or black **cover**.
- Side-saddle **habit** with black **riding boots**.
- **Shirt** with collar, and **tie** with plain bar **tie pin**.
- Leather **gloves**.
- **Cane** or **whip** not more than 75cm (30in) in length.

NOTE:
- Hair ribbons should be black, brown or navy blue only, and should be kept to a minimum.
- It is incorrect for children riding side-saddle in showing classes to wear a spur.

Ponies of Show Hunter Type and Working Hunter Ponies

- PAS 015 or EN 1384 **skull cap/riding hat**, correctly secured, with a dark blue or black cover.
- **Shirt** with collar, and **tie** with **stock pin**.
- Tweed **coat**. (Dark blue or black coats may be worn for final judging at major shows.)
- **Jodhpurs** (beige).
- **Jodhpur boots** (brown). For older children, plain **riding boots** with garter straps.
- **Cane** or **whip** not exceeding 75cm (30in) in length. Hunting whips are not permitted.

NOTE:
- Spurs are not permitted.

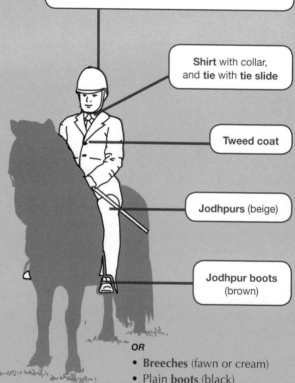

PAS 015 or EN 1384 **skull cap/riding hat**, correctly secured, with a cover that tones in with the colour of the coat. A jocket skull cap must be worn in working hunter pony classes.

Shirt with collar, and **tie** with **tie slide**

Tweed coat

Jodhpurs (beige)

Jodhpur boots (brown)

OR

- **Breeches** (fawn or cream)
- Plain **boots** (black)
- **Gloves** (string or leather)
- Leather-covered **show cane**

Mountain and Moorland Ponies

Under the rules of the British Show Pony Society (BSPS), the following apply:

- Correctly secured British Standard **skull cap/riding hat** numbers PAS 015/EN 1384, that meet current safety standards, must be worn by riders at all times when mounted.
- **Riding jacket**.
- **Shirt** with collar, and **tie** with plain bar **tie slide**, or collarless **shirt** with **hunting tie and stock pin**.
- **Breeches** or **jodhpurs**.
- **Riding boots** or **jodhpur boots**.

NOTE:
- Gaiters may be worn.
- Chaps are not permitted.
- A rider whose chin strap comes undone while competing must, on penalty of elimination, replace it or fasten it before continuing. The rider may stop without penalty to fasten the strap
- Waterproof jackets are permitted.
- Body protectors may be worn and are strongly recommended when competing in Working Hunter Pony classes.
- Earrings and body studs must not be worn.
- Mobile telephones and ear pieces must not be taken into the ring.
- The wearing of spurs in all classes held under BSPS rules is forbidden, except for riders aged 16 or over in horse classes, experimental intermediate classes and the exceeding 148cm Anglo- and Part-bred Arab classes.
- Whips are not to exceed 75cm (30in).n all classes held under BSPS rules,
- Hunting whips are permitted.

Side-Saddle

There are various competitions available to side-saddle riders, including show classes (*see* page 79), concours d'élégance and equitation classes. Generally speaking, correct side-saddle attire is acceptable in all these activities, but riders should study the rules of the Society under which individual competitions are run, to ensure that they comply with any special requirements.

The illustrated dress is correct for riders competing under The Side-Saddle Association rules for juniors (aged under 16 on the previous 1 January).

NOTE:
- In the case of small children, black or brown jodhpur boots are acceptable regardless of colour of habit.
- Plain gaiters may be worn, but not half-chaps.
- A spur or spur band is not permitted in any class where jumping is involved.
- Hair ribbons, if worn, to be plain black, brown or navy, and hair, however worn, should be exceptionally neat and tidy.
- Whip not to exceed 76cm when riding a pony not exceeding 148cm (14.2hh), or one metre when riding a horse/pony exceeding 148cm and of sufficient length to be used as a right leg aid.

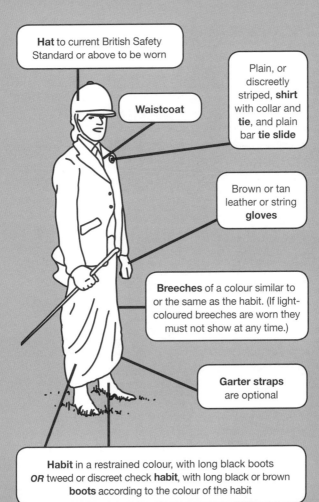

Hat to current British Safety Standard or above to be worn

Waistcoat

Plain, or discreetly striped, **shirt** with collar and **tie**, and plain bar **tie slide**

Brown or tan leather or string **gloves**

Breeches of a colour similar to or the same as the habit. (If light-coloured breeches are worn they must not show at any time.)

Garter straps are optional

Habit in a restrained colour, with long black boots *OR* tweed or discreet check **habit**, with long black or brown **boots** according to the colour of the habit

Additional Rules On Hats

DRESSAGE UNDER BRITISH DRESSAGE RULES

When competing in dressage run under the rules of British Dressage a hat, with the harness correctly fastened, must be worn at all times when mounted. All hats must be manufactured to one of the following minimum approved standards (or any new standard that meets or exceeds those stated):

- PAS 015, EN 1384, BSEN 1384 (British Dressage strongly recommends that hats are Kitemarked).
- ASTM F1163 (2004) with SEI mark.
- SNELL E2001.
- Australian and New Zealand All AS/NZS 3838 1988.

SHOWJUMPING UNDER BRITISH SHOWJUMPING RULES

All riders must wear protective headgear that includes a retaining harness secured to the shell at more than two points. Such headgear must be worn with the chinstrap properly adjusted and fastened when jumping in the arena, the practice area and the collecting ring.

It is mandatory for all Members to wear a protective helmet manufactured to EN 1384, ASTM F1163, PAS 015 or SNELL 2001 with Kitemark or SEI or such other protective headgear as affords a similar or higher level of protection and is at least that of EN 1384, ASTM F1163 or PAS 015.

EVENTING UNDER
BRITISH EVENTING RULES

Protective headwear, with the harness correctly fastened, must be worn by competitors at all times when mounted in BE80, BE90, BE100 and BE100 Plus classes. This rule applies to the dressage and showjumping phases as well as cross country. Protective headwear, which must show a visible BE hat tag, must meet one of the following standards:

- British All PAS 015, BSEN 1384. Provided they are BSI Kitemarked or SEI.
- European EN 1384. Provided they are BSI Kitemarked or SEI.
- American All SEI ASTM 95, ASTM F1163 2004 and SNELL E2001.
- Australian and New Zealand All AS/NZS 3838 2003.

Useful Contacts

The Pony Club
Stoneleigh Park
Kenilworth
Warwickshire
CV8 2RW

Telephone: 02476 698300
Website: www.pcuk.org

British Dressage
Stoneleigh Park
Kenilworth
Warwickshire
CV8 2RJ

Telephone: 02476 698830
Website: www.britishdressage.co.uk

British Eventing
Stoneleigh Park
Kenilworth
Warwickshire
CV8 2RN

Telephone: 0845 262 3344
Website: www.britisheventing.com

The Side Saddle Association
Telephone: 02476 545555
Website:
www.sidesaddleassociation.co.uk

British Showjumping
Stoneleigh Park
Kenilworth
Warwickshire
CV8 2LR

Telephone: 02476 698800
Website: www.
britishshowjumping.co.uk

British Show Pony Association
124 Green End Road
Sawtry
Huntingdon
Cambridgeshire
PE28 5XS

Telephone: 01487 831376
Website: www.
britishshowponysociety.co.uk

The British Horse Society
Abbey Park
Stareton
Kenilworth
Warwickshire
CV8 2XZ

Telephone:
02476 840500 /
0844 848 1666
Website: www.bhs.org.uk

The Pony Club Pocket Equine Dictionary

Compiled by Judith Draper

ISBN 978-1-907279-10-2

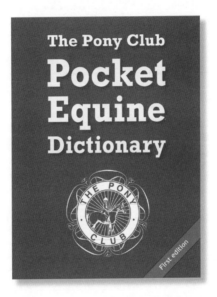

From ABSCESS to ZONKEY, *The Pony Club Pocket Equine Dictionary* clearly explains overy 500 equine words and terms in a clear, straightforward way. With a pocket-friendly size, it is the perfect companion for any young person keen to increase their understanding of the wonderful world of ponies and horses.

The Pony Club Pocket Guide to Equestrian Dress
has been compiled by renowned equestrian writer
Judith Draper, who for many years covered major
horse shows and events for national newspapers
and international magazines. She is the author of
many books, including **The Pony Club Pocket
Equine Dictionary**, **The Book of the Horse** and the
successful children's series **My First Pony**, **My First
Pony Care**, and **My First Pony Show**.

Also published by The Pony Club:

The Manual of Horsemanship
The Instructor's Handbook
The Pony Club Pocket Equine Dictionary
Building Show Jumping Courses
Keeping a Pony at Grass
Junior Road Rider
To Be a Dressage Rider
A Young Person's Guide to Eventing
Pasture Management
The *Stablemates* series: Vital Statistics; Body Basics;
    Fit for the Bit; All Systems Go!
Quiz Books 1, 2 and 3
Sticker Books 1, 2 and 3
The Pony Club Activity Book
'Look...No Hands!'—Straightforward Cross-Country
Design and Doodle with The Pony Club
So You Want to Buy a Pony?

**Visit The Pony Club's website for more information
about all Pony Club publications. *www.pcuk.org***